Building a Catspaw Dinghy
at East Hill Boat Shop

The Story in Pictures

ISBN 978-0-9802157-4-8

First Edition © 2013 by Jonathan James Books
Second Edition © 2013 by Jonathan James Books

Published in the United States of America
By Jonathan James Books, Middlesex, NY 14507

Appreciation for personal photo opportunities are due to Sterling Klinck,
builder of wooden boats at East Hill Boat Shop,
the Rochester Folk Art Guild, Middlesex, NY 14507

Jonathan James Books

To the "something more" found in finely handcrafted work

To the reader:

Boats without motors are boats that are moved by the strength of muscle or the power of the wind. People who use these boats are "quiet water people", people who listen for the sounds of the dip, dip, and swing of a canoe paddle cutting through a placid lake. Or the sound the oarlocks make when the oars are returned to start another stroke moving a rowboat ever closer to a favorite fishing spot. Or they would rather hear the waves lapping up against the hull of a sailboat over the background sound of wind filled sails. They would rather hear these sounds than listen to the roar of a large inboard engine or even the quiet putt—putt—putt of a small outboard motor clamped to the stern of a rowboat..

People who would rather ride in boats without motors get out onto the water, making hardly a sound and leave no big wakes behind them to crash against a quiet shore. Traveling without motors, these people tend to be more watchful of the movement of the wind and the water to help them get them where they want to go. And where they want to go may be no place except out on the water, away from the shore. Out on the water they can look back at the shore and feel for a moment they've left their life on land and can look at the world from a different point of view.

When he sails, a sailor can forget about the problems and worries that were nagging him before hoisting the mainsail. Once he is out on the water his mind clears and he watches the wind as it makes itself known by the ripples racing across the lake. When it's enough of a wind he can ride out over the water opposite the lean of the boat, pulling the mainsail tighter until he can see the keel cutting through the water underneath him. There's no thinking then, it's just being there, moving through the water with the wind and the boat.

The Catspaw Dinghy

The Catspaw Dinghy is Joel White's 10% expansion of Nat Herrshoff's well known Columbia Dinghy from the 1890's. The Catspaw is 12 ft 8 inches overall and White added a 63 sq ft sprits'l and centerboard. The Catspaw featured here was built by master craftsman and boat builder Sterling Klinck at East Hill Boat Shop, a part of the Rochester Folk Art Guild, Middlesex, New York. The boats there are built by hand using traditional wood working techniques and boat building methods. Specifications of the Catpaw remains true to White's design, with a few minor non-structural modifications such as additional seating built into the boat

This visual review of the building of a Catspaw is not intended to cover how to build a Catspaw from beginning to end, rather it's to give you a better idea of what it takes to build a Catspaw Dinghy by hand. When a boat is built by hand, there's a chance that the craftsman will build something more into the boat than the wood, paint, and nails which you can see. This "something more" makes it different than other boats. With great care and attention to even the smallest details, these Catspaw Dinghies are handcrafted together in a way which connects them to a living tradition of boat building. A tradition which places great value on that "something more" which only a craftsman working with a love of his craft can put into his work.

The Catspaw is a lovely boat with very sweet lines and should serve a person who would rather travel in a boat without motor for years to come.

May you have the wind forever at your back, the sun and fair weather clouds overhead, and a steady breeze to fill your sail.

-Jonathan James

#3 pattern

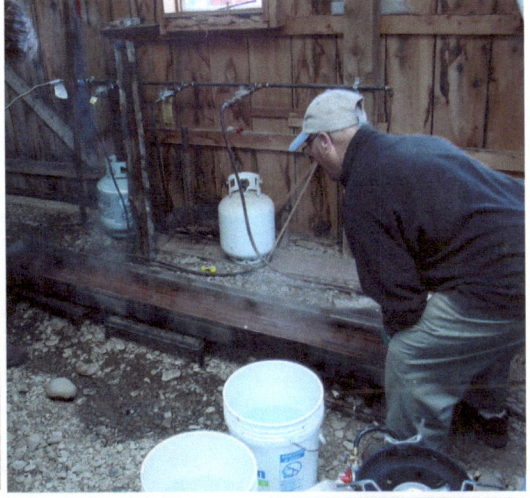

EAST HILL BOAT SHOP

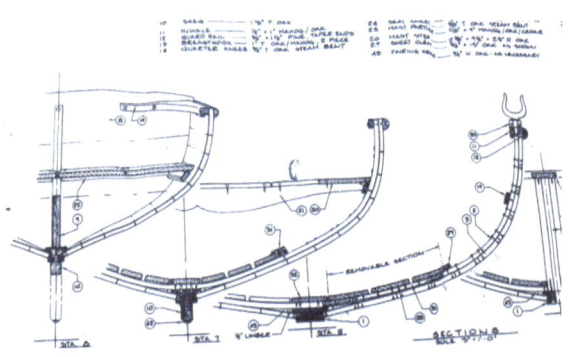

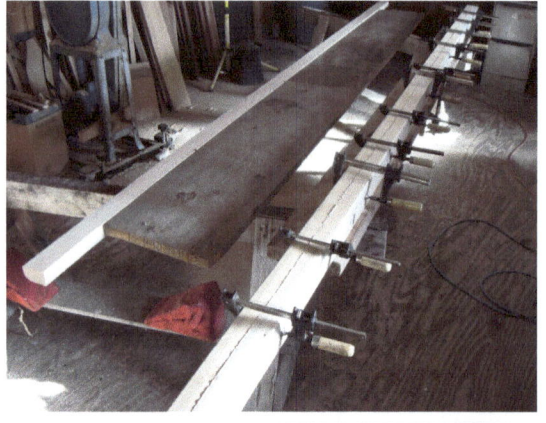

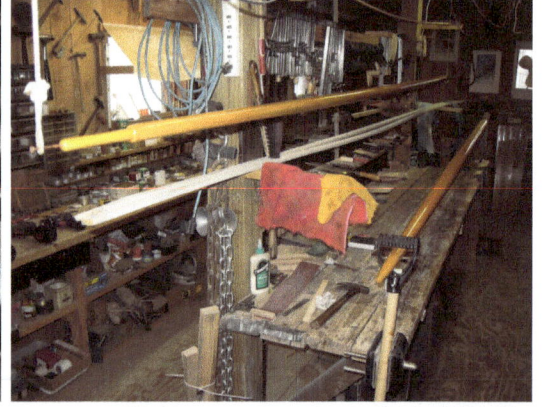

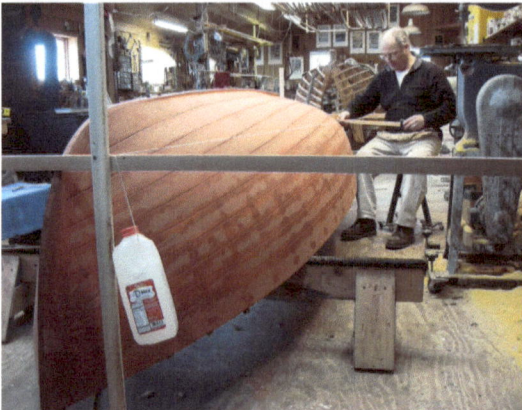

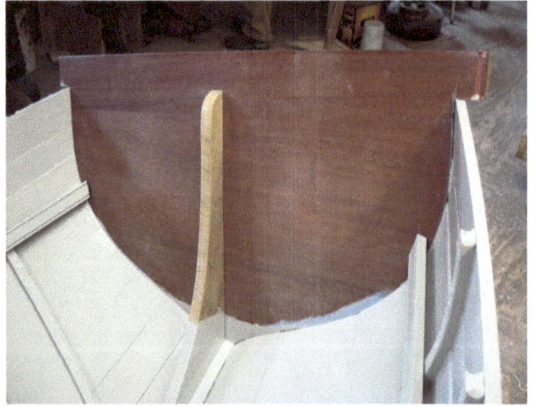

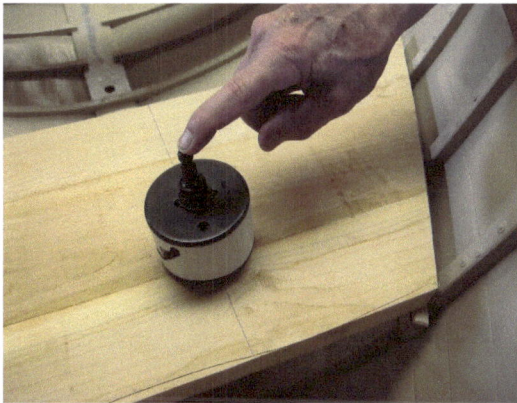

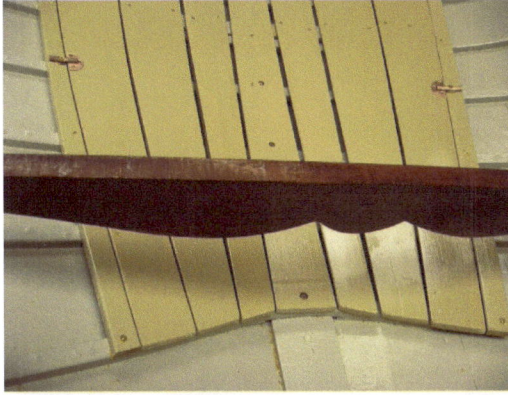
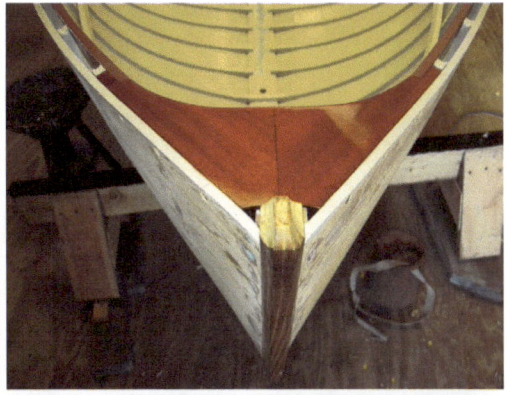

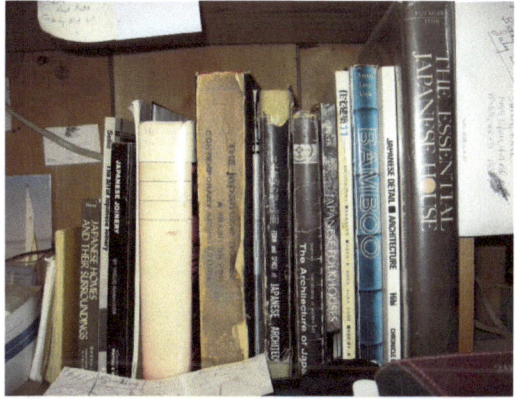

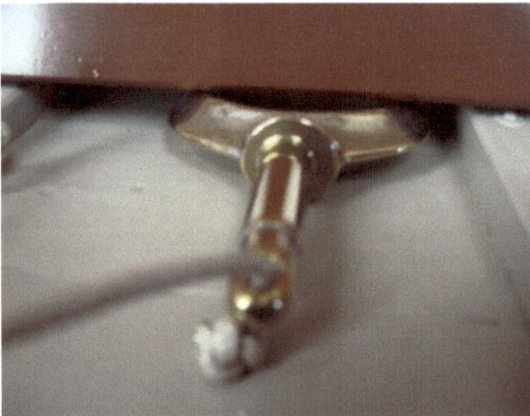

33

...and that's how the catspaw dinghy is built at East Hill Boat Shop.

Now it's time for someone to take the boat out on the water, someone who would rather travel on a boat without a motor. While the fine craftsmanship of the build can be seen in the boat shop, it's when the boat is being used that "something else" about it comes alive. Whether the dinghy is used for a daytime outing, or just to get away from the shore, when the boat is sailed the "something more" the craftsman built into the dinghy can be felt and appreciated for generations to come.

The End

Other books written and illustrated by Jonathan James

A Playful Dance—a book of children's poems for grownups and children, 2nd edition, ISBN 978-0-9802157-9-3

Listen to my song - a book of poems and nonsense musing, ISBN 978-0-980215-8-6

When I was but a youth—a book of poetic prose and nonsense musing for children who never grew up, ISBN 978-0-9802157-6-2

Jonathan James Books

Available through the Rochester Folk Art Guild, Middlesex, NY, 14507 (folkartguild.org) or through fine book stores everywhere.